DUBAI — LIFE & TIMES

DUBAI
LIFE & TIMES

Through the lens of Noor Ali Rashid

MOTIVATE
PUBLISHING

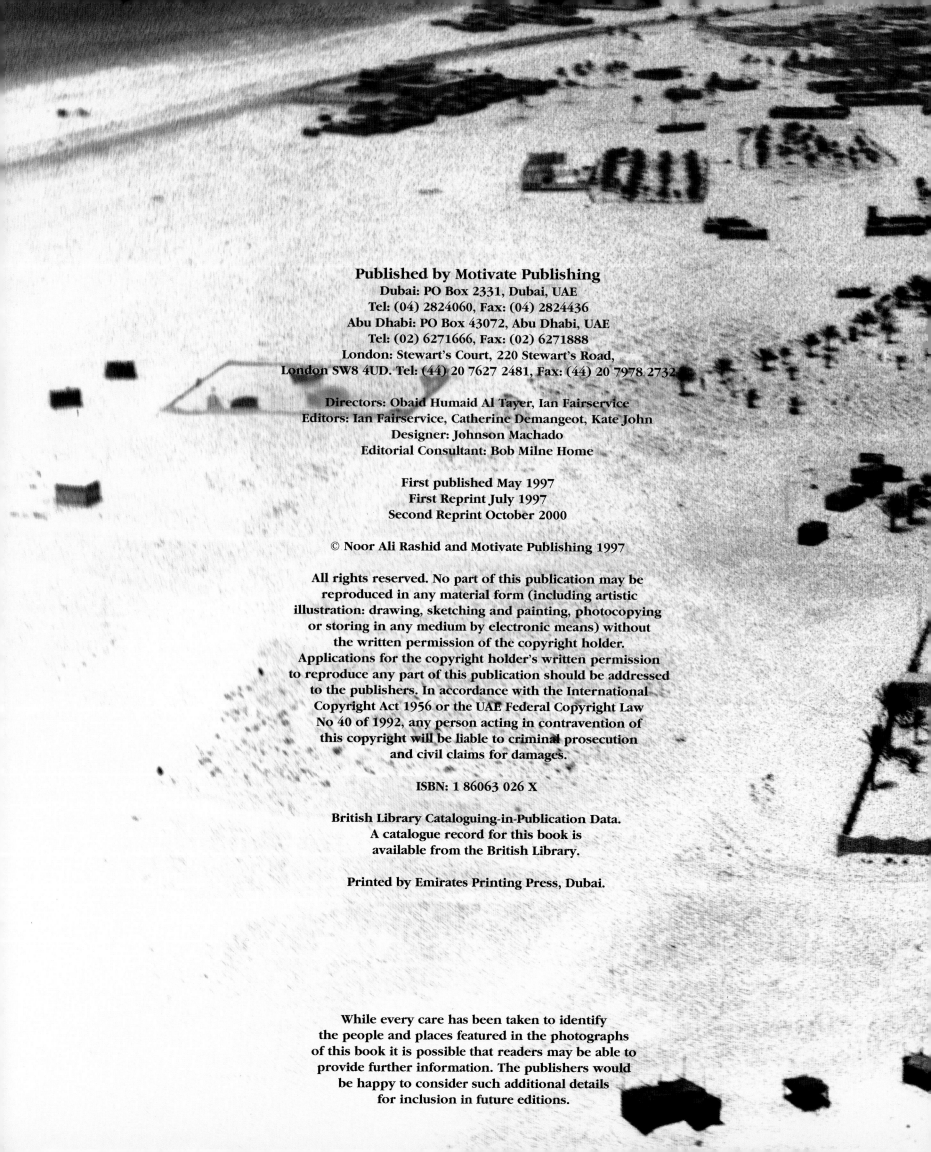

Published by Motivate Publishing
Dubai: PO Box 2331, Dubai, UAE
Tel: (04) 2824060, Fax: (04) 2824436
Abu Dhabi: PO Box 43072, Abu Dhabi, UAE
Tel: (02) 6271666, Fax: (02) 6271888
London: Stewart's Court, 220 Stewart's Road,
London SW8 4UD. Tel: (44) 20 7627 2481, Fax: (44) 20 7978 2732

Directors: Obaid Humaid Al Tayer, Ian Fairservice
Editors: Ian Fairservice, Catherine Demangeot, Kate John
Designer: Johnson Machado
Editorial Consultant: Bob Milne Home

First published May 1997
First Reprint July 1997
Second Reprint October 2000

ISBN: 1 86063 026 X

British Library Cataloguing-in-Publication Data.
A catalogue record for this book is
available from the British Library.

Printed by Emirates Printing Press, Dubai.

While every care has been taken to identify
the people and places featured in the photographs
of this book it is possible that readers may be able to
provide further information. The publishers would
be happy to consider such additional details
for inclusion in future editions.

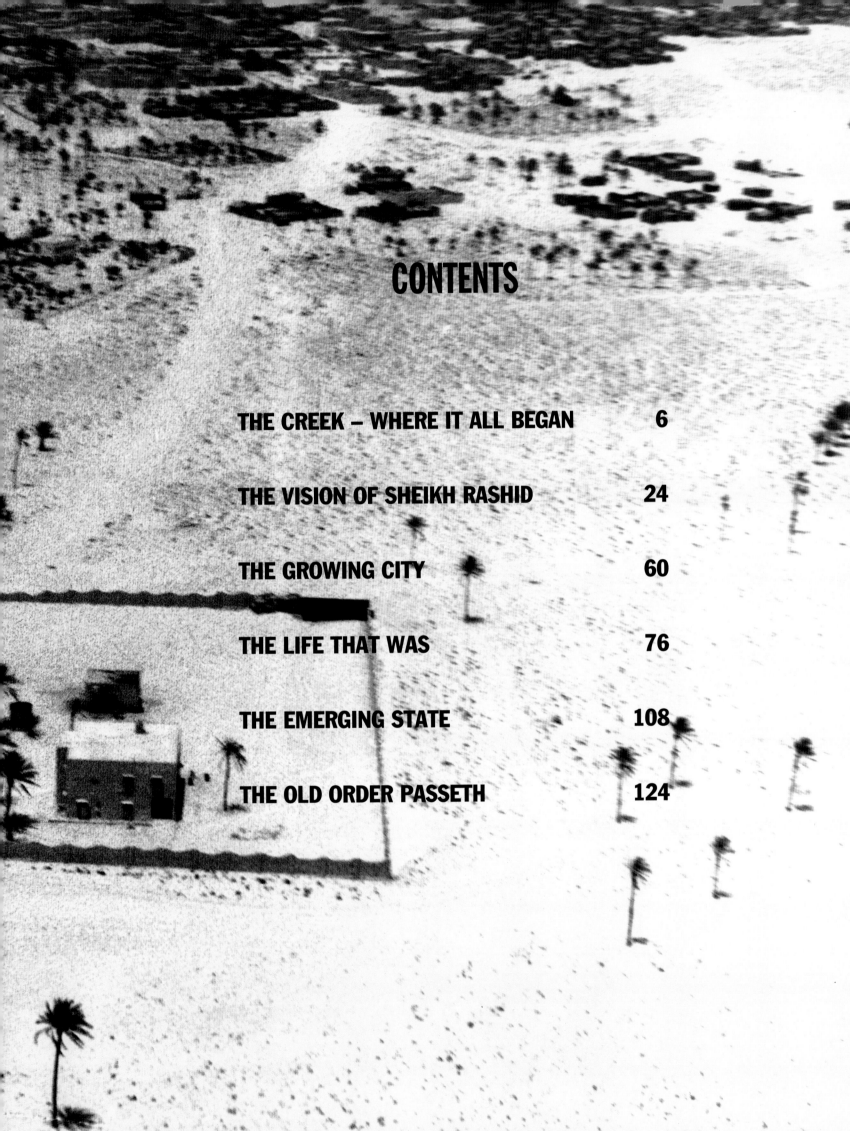

CONTENTS

THE CREEK
WHERE IT ALL BEGAN

Previous pages: Dubai creek – the reason for the city's existence. Rooftop aerials and a few modern buildings hint at the changes to come but, for the most part, in 1961, the banks of the waterway were still lined, as they had been for a century or more, only by the old wind-towered houses.

Most of the old buildings have gone, the wharfage has been improved, the Bedford trucks have been replaced by Nissans and Toyotas, and the abras now have powerful motors rather than oars – but the dhows have hardly changed at all and still make their voyages to the ports of the Gulf, the Indian subcontinent and East Africa.

WHILST THERE HAD been a settlement on the site of present-day Dubai for centuries, the city's modern history began in 1833 when a branch of the Bani Yas family of Abu Dhabi, led by Obaid bin Said and Maktoum bin Buti, left Abu Dhabi to settle in Dubai. Attracted by the creek, a rare haven on the southern shores of the Arabian Gulf, the small community of some 800 souls lived by trading in fish and pearls. It was a modest existence, but it established Dubai as an entrepôt port and formed a secure basis for the commercial development that was to come – and still continues today. The town received a further boost to trade in the early years of this century when its practical fiscal policies found appeal with the merchants of the Persian ports on the eastern coast of the Gulf, who were disenchanted with new customs duties imposed by the Shah. In a fine demonstration of the effect of punitive taxation, they moved lock, stock and barrel (an appropriate analogy, since trade in firearms also formed an important part of the commercial activities) to the more congenial environment of Dubai. Now, nearly a hundred years later, multinational businesses are doing the same – and for much the same reason.

The ubiquitous Land Rover – along with the Bedford truck – formed a vital part of the logistics system. Roads were still uncommon – the first in Dubai was constructed in 1964 and it was not until 1967 that there was a surfaced link to Sharjah – so four-wheel-drive vehicles were essential.

A prime site on the banks of the creek in the mid-60s, at which time the Carlton Tower was built. As oil revenues began to come in there was a frenzy of construction as the infrastructure was built to meet the developing needs of the fast-expanding city. Just a few years before, children had played on the creek's sandy foreshores, where now there rose modern buildings.

Dubai was also a stopping point for Muslims from India and Pakistan on their way to Mekkah for performing Haj. These passengers seem to be viewing their impending voyage with some trepidation – or maybe it is the thought of boarding along that narrow, unstable gangplank that is the cause of their apparent anxiety.

IN THE LATE 1950s the creek, the city's lifeline for trade, was beginning to silt, and the currents that sweep along the Gulf coast were piling sandbars across its mouth. Sheikh Rashid bin Saeed Al Maktoum, the then Ruler, arranged to borrow US$960,000 – a considerable sum at any time and particularly so in those pre-oil days – to dredge the waterway and construct breakwaters at its mouth. During the 1960s the creek was narrowed – an exercise that not only allowed the faster flow of tidal water (which scoured the bed and helped to keep it free of silt) but also allowed land on the banks to be profitably reclaimed.

By this time Dubai was able to handle dhows of up to 500 tons and – since Sharjah's creek had also silted but remained undredged – there was a considerable increase in the volume of cargo handled at Dubai.

And not only cargo. Before aircraft became the main means of transport the dhows – and the fortnightly British India Steam Navigation Company service calling at Dubai en route from Bombay to Basra – were the usual methods by which passengers travelled to the emirate.

Overleaf: Like dhows and abras,
gulls are another constant
on the creek.

A dhow at anchor, waiting for a berth. Despite the dredging of the creek, larger vessels still had to anchor offshore and in 1967 the decision was taken by Sheikh Rashid to build a deep-water port.

Waiting for a fare on Dubai-side. The crossing between Shindaga and Ras was known as the two-anna abra – referring to the cost of the journey when the Indian currency was in use in Dubai. The alternative crossing point towards the creek's mouth was known as the four-anna abra, which was worth a quarter of a rupee.

PASSENGERS BOARDING VESSELS on the creek were not always destined for long ocean voyages. Whilst both sides of the waterway are now integral parts of one city, for over one hundred years Dubai and Deira were separate entities, the latter being ruled by Sheikhs who had defected from Sharjah. Sheikh Rashid reunited the two politically in the early 1950s, but the creek remained a physical barrier. Until the construction of the Maktoum Bridge in 1963 – and subsequently the Shindaga tunnel and a further bridge at Al Gharoud – travellers between Dubai and Deira faced either a lengthy journey through the treacherous *sabkha* and soft dunes around the head of the creek or a ride on an abra. These small water-taxis were, and still are, an essential link in the city's transport system – and a picturesque one too. Whilst daily commuters may take for granted the handsome views of the city that an abra ride offers, visitors are not so blasé – and at 50 fils per trip find it to be amongst the world's best sightseeing value.

The oars shaped like extended table-tennis bats were unusual. These were characteristic of the disembarking boats that were towed behind the dhows and used to ferry the crew and goods ashore.

Modern buildings are beginning to interrupt the original skyline of windtowers and minarets but even in the 1960s there were still many muscle-powered abras.

WHILST TRADING DHOWS formed the bulk of the traffic on the creek, there was plenty of other activity too, including shipbuilding and fishing – and the traditions of both are still continued today.

The raw materials for the building of these sturdy vessels, then as now, were imported from India, especially from Calicut. For centuries skilled shipwrights – without the aid of formal plans or blueprints and using just saws, bowstring drills and hammers – had been constructing these and other boats on the foreshores of the Gulf. Yet these apparently haphazardly-fabricated vessels were capable of long ocean voyages and enabled Arab merchants to extend their trading links to India, Africa, south-east Asia and China. The maritime tradition continues – but now includes repair of supertankers in one of the world's largest dry dock complexes.

The warm waters of the Gulf provide a plentiful harvest of fish – including sailfish, shark, marlin, bonito, snapper, hammour, mackerel, anchovy and sardines – which formed an important part of the diet of the inhabitants of the region. The most productive season is between September and May, when the nutrient-rich and less salty waters of the Indian Ocean flow into the Gulf.

Boat building on the foreshore near the Maktoum Bridge. Dhows are still built in Dubai at a site only a few hundred metres from this one, whilst further along the creek modern yards tend oil support vessels and coastal trading ships.

Trap nets piled high aboard dhows bound for the fishing grounds are still a familiar sight. Then as now, the catches were delivered twice daily to the fish market.

In the mid-1960s, Dubai was a town on the brink of change. Dhows still cluster along the shore, most buildings are still of just one or two storeys and the desert is clearly visible just a kilometre or so away. But a swathe of tarmac can be seen and the reshaping of the mouth of the creek is well under way.

The fruit and vegetable markets were more permanently settled. Whilst some of the produce was grown locally, much was imported, either by sea or, as the road network was developed, by truck.

IMPORTED GOODS WERE unloaded from arriving vessels and carried by handcart or wheelbarrow through the busy streets to Dubai's main souks, located close to the creek. In common with most Arab towns each market dealt in a particular commodity and, as is still the case today, provided a feast for the senses – in the aromatic scent of spices, the more pungent aromas of the fish souk, and the heady fragrances of perfumes; in the kaleidoscopic confusion of colours in the fabric market and the gleam of precious metals and jewels in the gold souk.

Retailing was a simpler affair in those days. Many shops were simply a rug placed on any spare bit of ground, whilst others – the more sophisticated – had counters made of old packing cases and shade provided by sacking. All very different to the air-conditioned malls enjoyed by today's shoppers.

Women gather to sell home-produce, consisting of small cheeses, labneh and riqa (flat bread) and ghee in jars. Also amongst their wares were all varieties of cosmetic items, from kohl powder to herbal medicines.

Aboard the crowded vessel, passengers are pictured here making the most of trading an odd assortment of goods. Any items left unsold when the passengers came ashore would then be traded on the banks of the creek.

WHILST CIVIL DEFENCE and policing had been the responsibility of the Ruler's guards in the towns – and, since the early 1950s, that of the Trucial Oman Scouts in rural districts – the growth of the cities, the escalating population and the arrival of motor cars in increasingly large numbers required a more formal approach to the organisation of such community matters as emergency services and the enforcement of law and order. It was perhaps this that most definitively marked the transition from the old way of life, in which everybody knew everybody, to a modern society in which the population increasingly relies upon the assistance of professional services.

Fire, perhaps the greatest fear of seamen, is a particular hazard in wooden boats. Insurance of dhows and their cargoes was not usual in the 1960s – and this vessel, despite the attempts of the firefighters and brave volunteer boat owners, was a total loss.

Boarding along narrow gangplanks, a feat that required all the balancing skills of a circus high-wire act, was often hazardous. It was not uncommon for a passenger's possessions – and sometimes the passenger himself – to end up in the water. Here a traveller's goods are spread out to dry after an impromptu immersion.

Before the construction of wharves many goods were unloaded into abras or carried ashore – unless the cargo could be persuaded to be winched into the creek. Pictured here a crew member from Pakistan leads an ox to the shore, while the process of winching additional herd from the boat begins again. Such arcane methods were not to last for long: during the 1960s quays and warehouses sprang up along the banks of the creek, speeding the loading and unloading of cargoes.

EVEN IN PRE-OIL days Dubai was already thriving, its creek filled with vessels and its merchants prospering. Low customs duties are often cited as the reason for Dubai's success – and undoubtedly they played a part in the development of the city as the region's leading entrepôt port. However, it is nonetheless true that Dubai's commerce flourished with a standard rate of duty of four and five-eighths per cent – reduced in 1973 to three per cent – whilst in Abu Dhabi trading activities languished despite a general rate of just two and a half per cent being applied.

Although agriculture has always been an important industry in the UAE, with less than five per cent of the total land area suitable for normal cultivation – and even then relying on careful tapping of the limited underground water resources and the scant winter rainfall – many foodstuffs, as well as nearly all manufactured items, had to be imported. And, in keeping with Dubai's trading ethos, profitably re-exported too.

By the late 1960s the creek was hosting oil support vessels, luxury cruisers and speedboats. On land, surfaced roads, street lamps and air-conditioned concrete buildings were beginning to replace the sandy alleys, date palms and wind-towered houses. But the dhows and the abras remained – as, happily, they do today.

The waters of the creek that at night had for so long reflected only the fitful light of oil lamps and torches found new illumination with the introduction of electricity to Dubai in 1952 – appropriately enough in the form of lamp-posts at the abra stations.

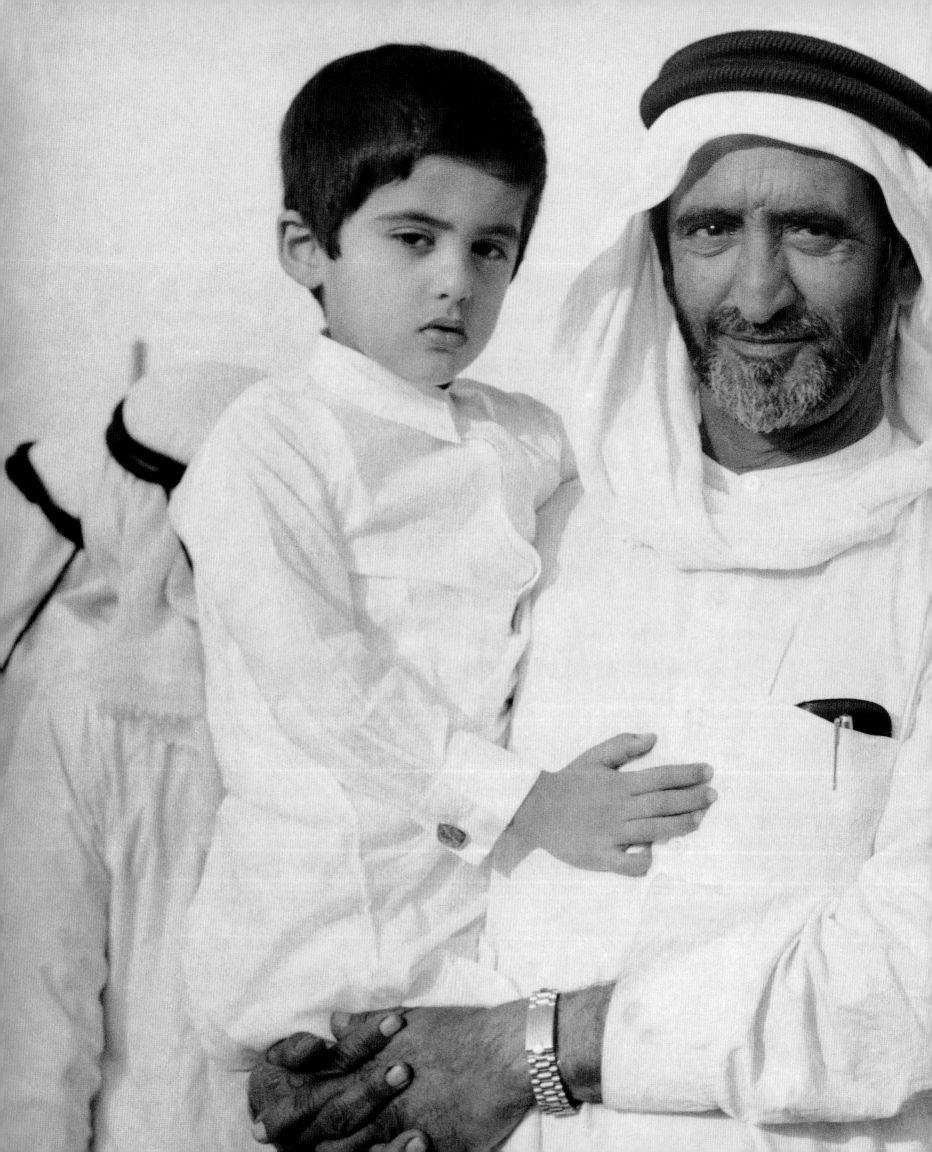

THE VISION OF SHEIKH RASHID

Watching a joint display by the military and police bands of the Gulf: Sheikh Mohammed, Kenneth Timbrell, Julian Bullard, Sheikh Rashid, Jack Briggs, Sheikh Maktoum and Sheikh Hamdan – as well as the gentleman on the roof.

Previous pages: Sheikh Rashid with his grandson, Sheikh Mansoor bin Ahmed Al Thani, son of Sheikh Ahmed bin Ali Al Thani, former Ruler of Qatar, at the close of a horse-race, of which Sheikh Mohammed was the winner.

COMMERCIAL ACUMEN IS undoubtedly a Maktoum family trait. In 1900, when the Bombay & Persian Navigation Company requested port facilities at Sharjah, Sheikh Rashid's grandfather, Sheikh Maktoum bin Hasher, let it be known that the company's sailors were infamous for the depths of their depravity and dissolution. Whilst the Ruler of Sharjah, disturbed at the thought of bands of drunken seamen roaming the streets of his town, pondered the matter, Sheikh Maktoum concluded an agreement whereby all of the shipping company's movements in the Gulf called at Dubai.

Sheikh Maktoum's son, Sheikh Saeed bin Maktoum ruled from 1912 to 1958 but, by 1939, Sheikh Rashid was, de facto, Regent. His astuteness, foresight and confidence – David Holden in his 'Farewell to Arabia' observed that Sheikh Rashid had learnt the tricks of trading at his father's knee – were to provide the impetus that propelled, even before the discovery of oil, Dubai's remarkable increase in prosperity.

Sheikh Rashid completing a business transaction with Mehdi Al Tajir while Sheikh Maktoum and Julian Bullard look on.

Resplendent in their uniforms, two Royal Navy officers with Donald Hawley and Sheikh Hamdan at an official luncheon hosted by Sheikh Maktoum at Zabeel Palace in the absence of Sheikh Rashid.

AT THE BEGINNING of 1968, after nearly a century and a half in the Gulf, the British had informed the leaders of the Trucial States that they would be withdrawing from the region in 1971. On 18 February, 1968 Sheikh Zayed and Sheikh Rashid had met at the village of As Sameeh on the border of the two emirates, where together they established the basis upon which the UAE would be founded – a union which they invited the Rulers of the other emirates, as well as those of Qatar and Bahrain, to join.

In the months that followed Sheikh Rashid and Sheikh Zayed met frequently, with the result that the years of planning were brought to a successful conclusion on 2 December, 1971 when the Rulers of the individual sheikhdoms formed the United Arab Emirates.

Sheikh Rashid and Sheikh Zayed meet at Zabeel, soon after the latter's accession as Ruler of Abu Dhabi in 1966. Diplomatic representatives of Her Majesty Queen Elizabeth II who also attended – pictured here stepping from the car in the background – were welcomed with the traditional ritual of incense.

Sheikh Rashid and Sheikh Saqr bin Mohammed Al Qassimi, the Ruler of Ras Al Khaimah, after a meeting of the Trucial States Development Council, of which Sheikh Saqr was the first chairman.

Attending the Rulers' meeting at Dubai's Political Agency during the early 1960s, from left to right – Sheikh Rashid; James Craig, Political Agent in Dubai; Sheikh Shakhbut; Colonel Boustead, Political Agent in Abu Dhabi; Sheikh Ahmed bin Rashid Al Mualla, the late Ruler of Umm Al Quwain; Sheikh Mohammed bin Hamad Al Sharqi, the late Ruler of Fujairah; another Commanding Officer, Trucial Oman Scouts; Sheikh Saqr bin Sultan Al Qassimi, former Ruler of Sharjah; Sheikh Saqr bin Mohammed Al Qassimi, Ruler of Ras Al Khaimah and Sheikh Rashid bin Humaid Al Nuaimi, the late Ruler of Ajman.

Sheikh Rashid's vision of Dubai was beginning to take physical shape. Where dhows had previously had to moor in mid-creek, wharves now enabled quicker, safer loading and unloading – and the developing road system allowed for swifter distribution of goods. This aerial view shows the new Ruler's office, appropriately built in close proximity to the trading heart of the city.

ALTHOUGH A LOCAL council was set up in 1957 it was really Sheikh Rashid's commissioning of an overall town plan in 1959 that led to the establishment of Dubai Municipality in 1961. With Sheikh Hamdan as chairman the Municipality was to become the main agent in Dubai's rapid and well-planned expansion, its varied activities including issuing of trading licences; control of public health; mapping and planning the city's building programme; co-ordinating electricity, telephone, water and sewage works; administering the ambitious schemes for planting parks and gardens; and registering land ownership.

Whilst many of its functions have now been taken over by ministries, the Municipality remains a powerful force in the running of the city.

Sheikh Rashid's visit to the Land Department in 1961, for which Sheikh Maktoum was responsible. Posing for posterity: front row from the left, Sheikh Maktoum, Sheikh Rashid, Donald Hawley, Bill Duff, Ahmed Awad; back row from the left, Abdul Wahid Rostamani (second), Ismail Buhumaid (third) and Qasim Sultan (fifth).

A Dubai Municipality public health inspector examines the contents of a baker's shop.

A delegation of visiting businessmen from Europe pose for a picture with members of the Dubai Chamber of Commerce and Industry presided by Mohammed Saeed Al Mulla (first row, third from left). Also present were Juma Al Majid, Sultan Al Owais, Saif Ahmed Al Ghurair, Ahmed bin Sulayem, Nasr bin Abdul Latif, Mohammed Abdullah Al Qaz, Mohammed Hadi Badia; Hashem Khoory, Ahmed Al Lootah, Maghanlal Jethanand and Rahma Al Shamsi.

DUBAI'S CHAMBER OF Commerce, established in 1965, was the first in the Trucial States. From the outset it was given wide-ranging responsibility for the regulation of trade as well as advising the government on commercial legislation – resulting in a trading environment in which bureaucracy is kept at a level which avoids any unnecessary interference but ensures an equitable framework within which business may be properly conducted. Amongst the first recommendations made by the Chamber was that anybody issuing a cheque which was subsequently dishonoured due to insufficient funds should be liable to immediate arrest. Still in force today, the law has played an important part in ensuring a fair and disciplined business environment.

Naif Police Station during the Political Resident's routine inspection of the various departments run and often funded by the British. From left to right, a duty policeman; Khalifa Al Naboodah; Ahmed Hadid Al Ghaith; Peter Lorimer, Chief of Police; Sir William Luce, Political Resident of Bahrain.

SHEIKH RASHID REALISED that whilst the construction of roads, offices, low-cost housing and other facilities was important, a successful business environment also required a whole range of ancillary services – especially banking.

The first bank to open in Dubai was the British Bank of the Middle East which commenced operations here in 1946 and held a monopoly position until the National Bank of Dubai was founded in 1963. For most of the century the Indian rupee had been the currency in use in the Trucial States but when the rupee was devalued in 1966 Dubai established a joint currency with Qatar. It was not until 1973 that the UAE Currency Board (later to evolve into the Central Bank of the UAE) was set up to establish the national currency. International banks soon realised the potential and by 1974 there were 19 foreign banks operating in the UAE as well as seven locally incorporated institutions.

Sheikh Rashid in discussion with Hamad Al Futtaim, a leading Dubai businessman and close friend.

Sheikh Rashid with his uncle, Sheikh Hasher Al Maktoum and Jasim Al Midfa of Citibank, then known as First National City Bank. Sheikh Rashid concentrates on signing a cheque, a task he always carried out with great promptness.

Sheikh Rashid with Abdullah Mohammed Saleh, Managing Director of the National Bank of Dubai, and Mohammed Saeed Al Mulla, during the opening ceremony of the National Bank of Dubai.

Sheikh Rashid and Nasir bin Abdul Latif Al Serkal, a leading businessman of Dubai, seated together on the porch of Zabeel Palace during the evening majlis. Sheikh Rashid used to hold three majlises daily, where anyone could come to obtain the resolution of a conflict, the go-ahead for a new venture, or simply to keep in touch with the news.

DUBAI'S OIL WAS first struck, 90 kilometres offshore and 2,300 metres deep, on 6 June, 1966, but it was not until 1972 that exports commenced. Apart from Dubai Petroleum Company's imposing offices, some rig-building yards – now moved – that stood along the creek, and the comings and goings of support vessels there has never been much visible evidence of the oil industry in the city, simply because the oil itself does not come ashore.

Instead of installing costly pipelines from field to shore storage tanks and thence to a deep-water loading bay, the crude is stored at sea in *khazzans*, vast containers the shape of upturned champagne glasses that stand on the sea-bed, their tops protruding above the waves. Weighing 15,000 tons and with a capacity of some 20 million gallons, each *khazzan* has a diameter of 82 metres and a height of 62 metres. The principle is simple: because oil and water do not mix – and oil floats on water – crude is pumped into the *khazzan*, displacing the sea-water; tankers then remove the oil from the top of the *khazzan*, the sea-water rising accordingly.

The *khazzans* were assembled in Jumeirah from components manufactured in America by the Chicago Iron and Steel Company – whose huge crane that towered over the site was emblazoned with the company's name. Which is why one of Dubai's most popular beach resorts bears the appellation of a mid-western American city.

Officials of Dubai Petroleum Company demonstrate the workings of a khazzan to Sheikh Rashid.

WITH OIL REVENUES to finance the development of Dubai's infrastructure, Sheikh Rashid set about providing the facilities and services that would enable the city to further expand its commercial activities. Sheikh Rashid had already amassed a team of experts in a wide variety of different disciplines, both local people and foreigners – many of the latter making the city their home and who are still here after, in some cases, nearly 50 years. Around the emirate all the appurtenances of modern society began to appear – water supplies and sewage disposal, electricity, schools, medical and emergency services, policing, roads, telephones, ports, airport, offices, homes, parks and gardens, industrial sites and hotels.

Among old friends, from the left: Eric Tulloch, George Chapman, John Harris, Neville Allen, Bill Duff and their respective spouses gather to share a wealth of memories.

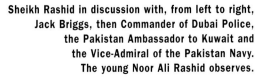

After a good day's photographic assignment, Noor Ali Rashid found great pleasure in sitting and relaxing with Sheikh Rashid, a man to whom he pledged the highest respect and warmest friendship.

Sheikh Rashid in discussion with, from left to right, Jack Briggs, then Commander of Dubai Police, the Pakistan Ambassador to Kuwait and the Vice-Admiral of the Pakistan Navy. The young Noor Ali Rashid observes.

SHEIKH RASHID'S VISION for the future of Dubai took on solid form with amazing rapidity. The creek was first bridged in 1963, again in 1974, and tunnelled under in 1975; a new port was opened in 1971, its 140 hectares of sheltered water enclosed by breakwaters constructed of three million tons of rock and 28,000 pre-cast concrete tetrapods each weighing 15 tons; a new terminal building was opened at Dubai International Airport in 1971 and the runway was extended to enable the operation of any type of aircraft; the then world's largest dry dock was completed in 1977; the 33-storey Trade Centre complex, at the time the tallest building in the Middle East, opened for business in 1979; and everywhere roads were being laid, piped water was being supplied and electricity was being installed.

Watchman of the creek: Sheikh Rashid's vision for the future revolved around the enormous potential of this natural resource.

Sheikh Rashid at Khawanij. The area had been producing crops for many years – albeit on a limited scale. Now modern dry-land farming techniques and improved irrigation have substantially increased Khawanij's productivity and enabled it to support dairy and poultry farms.

Sheikh Rashid was frequently in the public eye, though often on a much less formal level than at official functions, when he drove around the city, inspecting the latest construction projects and talking personally to the professional teams involved.

DUBAI'S MASTER PLAN was soon realised thanks to Sheikh Rashid assuming the dual role of architect and financier. Through shrewd conceptualising, Sheikh Rashid was then able to implement his vision of changing the face of the emirate with a programme of infrastructural developments and industrial enterprise.

The fruits of his labours and those serving him, was a rapidly transformed city, yielded from the hands of a wise and caring leader. While to many onlookers, the dramatic face-change of their city, bound by tradition and simple living may have seemed daunting, it was evident that their Ruler was led by an enduring confidence, one that could project long-term benefits in the ensuing developments through a steady pace of planning and hard work.

Overleaf: Despite ongoing improvements to the creek, access was still limited to vessels of less than 800 tons – and trade was booming. Imports, which had totalled just US$7.2 million in 1958 had doubled by 1960 – and by the end of the decade had reached nearly US$200 million. The 1970s saw even more rapid growth – and Port Rashid was further extended. And, along the coast to the south-west of the city, the world's largest man-made harbour was taking shape at Jebel Ali.

One of Sheikh Rashid's frequent tours of the city to take a closer look at developments. Transported across the creek by trusty abra, he is here accompanied by Hamad Al Futtaim, Ali Gargash, Ahmed bin Sulayem and Juma Al Majid, sitting on the right.

CONSTRUCTED AT A cost of US$456,000, the Maktoum Bridge physically united the towns of Deira and Dubai in 1963 – as Sheikh Rashid had politically united them a little over a decade earlier. Journeys between the two halves were to be made even easier by the construction of the tunnel linking Shindaga on the Dubai side with Ras in Deira. The project entailed the diversion of the creek first to the Deira side whilst the Shindaga part was dug beneath the then dry land, before re-diverting the waterway back to its former course whilst the Ras half was dug. The US$19-million undertaking provided two two-lane traffic tunnels and a pedestrian walkway running about 20 metres below sea level, but less than a metre beneath the bed of the creek.

The official opening of the Maktoum Bridge, linking Dubai and Deira. Saving a journey of several hours around the head of the creek, the bridge, initially a single carriageway, was soon expanded to four lanes.

A view of Maktoum Bridge from the Deira bank towards the Dubai side. For crossing the bridge from Deira there was a toll tax of four annas which was abolished when oil was discovered.

Ancient and modern – the past meets the future on the Maktoum Bridge.

Maktoum Street in the throes of development.

Previous pages: The planners at Dubai Municipality
had done their job well and progressively the pattern
of roads around which the city's initial development
was to be based began to be transferred from
blueprint to reality.

WHILST THE CORE of the city was centred on the Ruler's office on the banks of the creek, other new landmarks were beginning to appear. The Clock Tower and the Flame Roundabout are still there, although now perpetually encircled by streams of traffic. At the time these pictures – and that on the preceding pages – were taken, McDermott's were setting up their yard between the Clock Tower and the creek, the Airline Centre was planned but ground had not yet been broken, and out where the Trade Centre was to rise there was a scattering of *ghaf* trees and little else. In the 1960s Dubai was still essentially a small town and the towering office blocks, glittering hotels and swathes of elegant villas of today were yet still part of the Ruler's dream in the future.

The Clock Tower dominates Deira's skyline, as a modest flow of traffic encircles it.

The Flame Monument, now one of the city's most recognisable landmarks, was built to commemorate Dubai's first oil exports.

Karama in 1970. The expanse of sand was about to be replaced by low-cost housing units. Sheikh Rashid's plans for the city required an influx of expatriate workers, and his blueprint also included an area for their accommodation.

THROUGHOUT THE TOWN there were rising new construction projects. At Karama ground was being broken for the huge development of high-quality, low-cost housing that was to be built to provide comfortable, affordable homes for the influx of expatriates, particularly from the Indian sub-continent, who were coming into the country. At Zabeel, amidst low, undulating dunes, the Ruler's palace, constructed back in the 1950s, was by now being encircled by a spreading urban landscape. And at Satwa, where there was little but a scattering of *barasti* huts, there began the initial phase of work that was to lead the suburb to become an important commercial, shopping and entertainment centre.

Zabeel Palace, once isolated, became a familiar point of passage on many a commuter's journey from Jumeirah to the city centre. Now the main roads bypass it once again.

It is said that if you cannot find what you need in Satwa then it probably doesn't exist. Hundreds of little shops supplying everything from car spares to bridal dresses, jewellery to fiery curries, sprang up here after the initial development of the area.

Palm trees silhouetted against the tranquillity of a desert sunset. In the early sixties Jumeirah's peaceful acres were yet to echo to the sound of pile-drivers and concrete mixers.

JUMEIRAH – THE WORD means 'beautiful' – is now one of Dubai's most desirable addresses. Archaeological investigations have proved that the ancients found it attractive too – there is evidence of a sizeable and settled Sassanian community that flourished here some 1,500 years ago, a way-station on the trade routes between Oman and Yemen in the south and the sophisticated civilisations of the Euphrates and Tigris valleys in the north. It must have been a prosperous little place – jewellery, ceramics and other evidence of elegant living have been found amongst the remains of a marketplace, governor's palace, hunting lodge and houses.

At the beginning of the 20th century such glories were long gone and Jumeirah was the abode of fishermen – until the guest palaces were built and expatriates discovered its miles of white sandy beaches.

When these khazzans were being constructed along Chicago Beach, no-one imagined that the same area would, some 30 years later, host a tourism and leisure resort of unparalleled luxury.

The single-carriageway Beach Road, without a car in sight, stretches invitingly up towards Chicago Beach.

DEREK NIMMO, THE British actor who has been visiting Dubai for some 20 years, asked a 1977 audience how they felt about living on a building site. The question was germane – the entire city seemingly devoted to reincarnating itself. Along the creek, where the elegant lines of the dhows had been supplemented by the squat barges and tugs used to ferry supplies to the offshore oil installations, the reclaimed land sprouted hotels, office blocks and apartment buildings.

Such was the demand for hotel accommodation that the Inter-Continental, Dubai's first five-star property, would, apocryphally anyway, offer visitors who were denied a room due to the chronic shortage of beds in the city, the opportunity of sleeping on chairs in the lobby for half price.

In 1978 the Sheraton Hotel, now upstaged by the spectacular architecture of the National Bank of Dubai and Chamber of Commerce buildings, dominated this section of the creek. Beyond it is the McDermott yard, where a variety of oil installations were constructed.

Noor's aerial photograph shows the Inter-Continental Plaza in the final stages of construction – it officially opened in May 1978. Beyond the hotel itself is the Dubai Municipality building, with its space-age design which, to this day, is admired by Dubai residents and visitors alike.

Still waters. Despite the manifest changes along its banks the creek retains its intrinsic charm. Dhows still ply its waters, small barges lie idle between shifts of pulling cargo, and abras still fuss back and forth. For a generation brought up amongst the benefits of modern Dubai, for whom the old, harder way of life is something they read about in history books or hear from their grandparents, the presence of the creek provides a link to their heritage.

WHILST FOR MANY states in the Arabian Gulf it was the discovery of oil that led to the abrupt transition from the old way of life to the new, there were additional reasons in Dubai. Because of the emirate's expertise in commerce – which has been both led and encouraged by the Maktoum family for over 150 years – its late entry into oil exports and, relative to other Gulf nations, its small output, much of the extraordinary progress of the last three decades has been due to the growth of its mercantile economy. The most prestigious example has been the establishment of the Dubai Shopping Festival, the world's largest event of this nature.

A creekside extravaganza of fireworks and laser shows launches the 1997 Dubai Shopping Festival, drawing huge crowds to view the many spectacles on display.

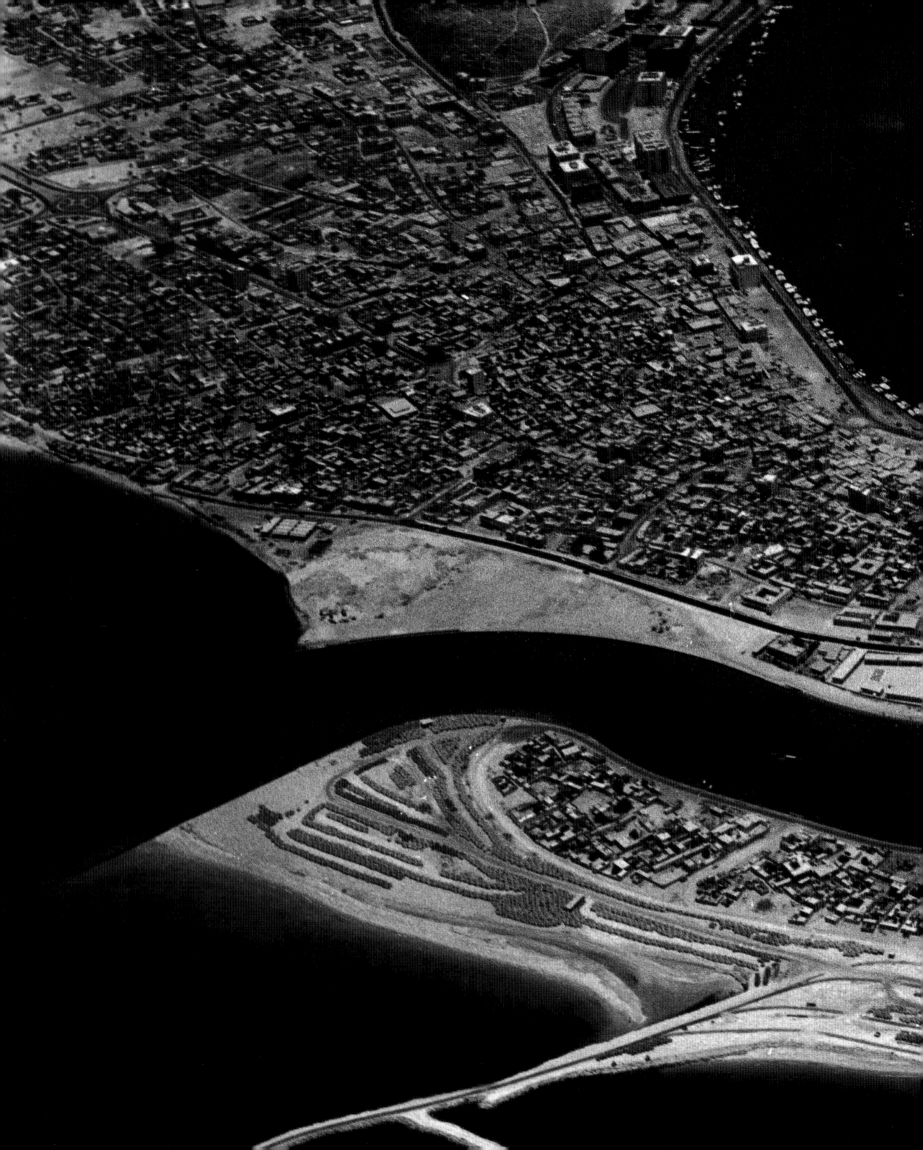

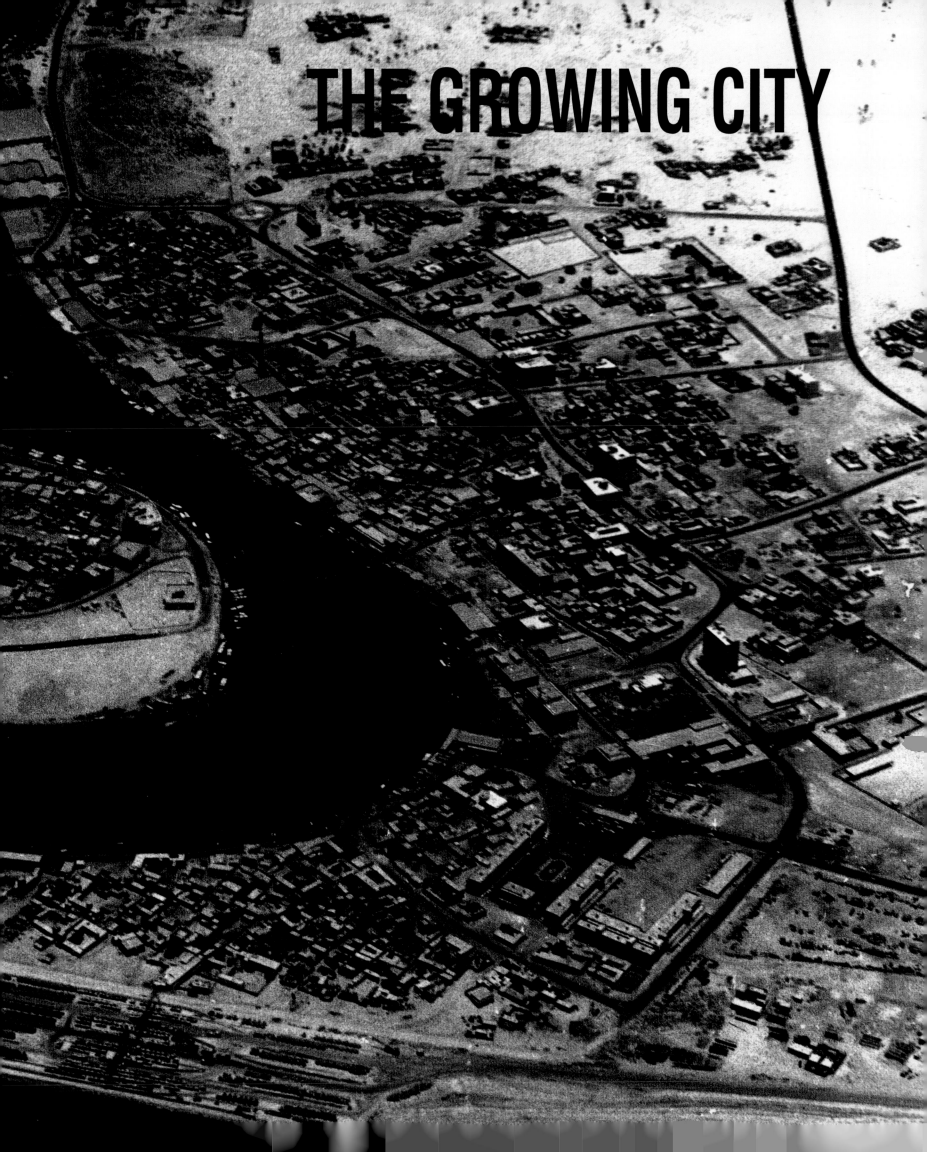

THE GROWING CITY

Warehouses, fork-lift trucks and ample roadways enabled Dubai to provide general cargo ships with swift, efficient turnrounds.

PORT RASHID, AT the time the largest port in the Gulf, enabled Dubai to provide, for the first time, a full range of modern services to ships and their cargoes. Installed with the latest handling equipment the port dramatically speeded up loading and unloading, as well as enabling the easy supply of fresh water, comprehensive provisions, bonded stores and bunkering. Initially opened with 16 berths, plans were immediately put in hand to bring the total capacity up to 37 berths, capable of handling vessels of up to 38' draught.

Until the construction of the port, vessels too large to be able to enter the creek were required to anchor offshore, whence their cargoes and passengers had to be transferred to lighters. Slow, inefficient and occasionally hazardous, the method had been adequate for the smaller amounts of cargo that had hitherto been destined for Dubai, but could not meet the rapidly expanding needs of a fast developing community.

Previous pages: Curving through the heart of the town, the creek has been described as giving Dubai something of the atmosphere of Venice. If one substitutes abras for gondolas, minarets for campaniles, car parks for piazzas and towering modern architecture for the more intricate styles of the Adriatic city, the comparison could just stand – but it really isn't necessary: Dubai is sufficiently attractive in its own right and doesn't require analogies.

In 1967 the first plans for Port Rashid called for just four deep-water berths – but even before they were completed their envisaged capacity had been overtaken by the rapid increase in traffic, from US$168 million in 1968 to US$194 million the following year.

Port Rashid under construction. Some of the 28,000 tetrapods that went to complete the breakwaters may be seen.

Sheikh Rashid, Sheikh Maktoum, Sheikh Saqr of Ras Al Khaimah, the British Political Agent and guests attending the piling ceremony at Port Rashid.

SO RAPID WAS the increasing demand for port facilities that it was decided to add yet further berths to Port Rashid as well as developing a completely new port at Jebel Ali. This, the largest man-made harbour in the world – so huge that its familiar key-shaped plan is reputedly visible from space – has now become an important industrial centre, companies from around the globe being attracted by its duty-free status, liberal employment laws and favourable financial climate.

The merchants of old, trading in pearls, gold and spices have now developed new business skills in industries as diverse as electronics, machinery and fast food; the erstwhile fishermen and farmers deal in commodities on a global basis; and traditional Arab hospitality finds expression in welcoming sun-seeking visitors – but despite the changes and developments the spirit of Dubai remains the same as ever. Any dhow captain from a century ago, whilst he would be amazed at the technical progress, would find the motive for a vessel's voyage – be it a bulk carrier or dhow, supertanker or coastal tramp – has remained precisely the same.

The Shell Jetty on the Deira side of the creek.

Sheikh Rashid, Prince Philip and Ahmed Baker watch approvingly as Britain's Queen Elizabeth II unveils a commemorative plaque at the official opening of Jebel Ali Port on February 26, 1979.

Sheikh Mohammed visits an onshore rig on the occasion of its erection. He is accompanied, from his left, by Humaid Al Tayer, Sheikh Omar bin Obaid Al Majid, Salem Musabah and Abdul Karim Takizadeh (Captain).

DUBAI'S INVESTMENT IN major capital projects such as the port and airport, the bridge across the creek and later the dry dock, Jebel Ali and the Trade Centre were not in response to the then needs of the community; rather they were in preparation for a future that many observers, less far-sighted than Sheikh Rashid, believed to be unrealisable. This deliberate policy of attracting business to the city through providing, in advance, the facilities needed has been continued ever since and then, as now, it is not the income from oil itself that has solely generated Dubai's economic growth. Wisely-used oil revenues combined with the tradition of successful trading have enabled the emirate to develop a much broader trading and industrial base than many other states in the region.

Sheikh Rashid holding a model of a khazzan.

THE CITY'S MERCHANTS had built their houses along the shores of the creek, from which convenient vantage points they could keep a watchful eye on the comings and goings of their vessels. With the arrival of banks (Dubai's first bank opened in 1946) it was logical that they should be near their customers – and the source of their customers' wealth.

The banks served the growing needs of their customers by providing what the region's merchants required: working capital with which they could finance and develop their businesses. The banks would take deposits and then lend sums for short-term finance of trade – most commonly by advances and import credits. Since the bulk of their lending was to local businessmen rather than expatriate firms, negotiations were customarily conducted on the basis of trust – to ask for security was tantamount to questioning a man's honour and, in many cases, there was little or nothing to be offered as collateral anyway.

The British Bank of the Middle East, now known as BritishBank, pioneered modern banking in the Arabian Gulf states – indeed it was the only bank in Dubai from 1946 to 1963.

Previous pages: Shipping queues offshore waiting to unload the raw materials that are needed to continue the city's growth. The road along the Deira bank does not yet stretch as far as Ras, but Maktoum Street is fully paved. Many of today's tall buildings around Nasr Square have yet to be built – and those in the foreground, new at the time, have now been demolished.

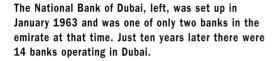

The National Bank of Dubai, left, was set up in January 1963 and was one of only two banks in the emirate at that time. Just ten years later there were 14 banks operating in Dubai.

An aquatic Wall Street. Good banks have always sited themselves close to the people and trades they serve.

BURGEONING BUSINESS WAS not exclusive to the construction industry. Other trades benefited from increasing prosperity – what modern economists would call the trickle-down effect – and new services were introduced to meet the needs of a progressively more sophisticated business community and demanding public.

Previously tides, seasons and day and night had dictated much of the business activity; now telephones, cars and air travel were to speed the pace of life in a way that would have been inconceivable just a generation earlier.

But not all change was immediate. In the souks the traditional methods of buying and selling continued – as to a very large extent they still do today. The elegant boutiques, speciality shops, department stores and air-conditioned malls that have made Dubai an internationally recognised centre for shopping were still a long way in the future.

An intriguing mixture of items is on offer at this stall, from children's toys and hubble-bubble pipes to baskets and incense burners. The little chap on the right in the enormous flip-flops seems to be studying his purchase with some intensity.

Apart from being able to buy just about anything in the souks it was also possible to get almost anything repaired – from a defective stereo to a worn-out shoe. Rough road surfaces played havoc with cycle tyres and repairers such as this gentleman were kept busy.

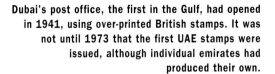

Dubai's post office, the first in the Gulf, had opened in 1941, using over-printed British stamps. It was not until 1973 that the first UAE stamps were issued, although individual emirates had produced their own.

WHILST NEW BUSINESSES and industries were rapidly being established, many of the old trades continued – albeit adapting to changing circumstances. Although pearling had declined almost to extinction during the 1930s, in the late '40s the Indian Government, in an attempt to stop the drain on the country's foreign exchange holdings, banned the importation of gold. The Government could not, however, eradicate the populace's desire for the metal, nor could it control the multi-million-dollar black market that it had created. Dubai's merchants, who had long established links with India through the pearl trade and were ever ready to take advantage of business opportunities, were quick to supply the need – an enterprise that was entirely legal until the dhows entered Indian waters.

As a result Dubai became one of the great world centres of the gold trade – and its gold souk is still one of the largest in the region. However, with inflation in the 1970s creating a global demand for the metal the price soared and it soon became beyond the reach of most Indians. Again, Dubai's merchants adapted to market changes, diversifying into the jewellery business.

Amidst the change some old industries continued. Ibrahim Al Fardan, a long-established pearl merchant – pictured here wearing a string of pearls on his wrist – and Sheikh Maktoum meet at a trade exhibition in Dubai.

At the first jewellery exhibition held at the Carlton Hotel, Dubai, Sheikh Maktoum is shown the detailed workmanship of a necklace from the well-known watch and jewellery firm, Ahmed Seddiqi & Sons. Also pictured: Majid Seddiqi, Hamid Seddiqi and Ibrahim Seddiqi.

THE LIFE THAT WAS

A way of life that was already fast disappearing when this photograph was taken. The collection of barasti huts would soon be swept away by the tide of modernisation and the wide, sandy main streets separating them marked the blueprint of new roads to come.

Teams of health inspectors from Dubai Municipality would regularly visit all areas of town, no doubt thankful for the go-anywhere ability of its fleet of Land Rovers.

APART FROM A very few streets that had been surfaced in Dubai there were no tarmac roads anywhere in the emirates until the link between Dubai and Sharjah was opened in 1967. Before then journeys between the two emirates could take hours. The trip from Dubai to Abu Dhabi was difficult even in summer when the *sabkha* was hard; in the winter when the occasional rains had fallen the route became a glutinous morass. And travellers who were headed from the Gulf coast to Fujairah usually made the journey by sea around the tip of the Musandam peninsula rather than attempt the trek through the mountains on tracks that could be passed only by camel, donkey or the sturdiest four-wheel-drive vehicles.

Clearly, if the people outside the towns were to benefit from the medical services, educational facilities and greater supply of goods that increased prosperity would bring, it would be necessary to embark on a major programme of road building.

Previous pages: Few modern buildings interrupted the skyline of windtowers and minarets in this photograph. Only the pitched roofs of recently-built warehouses hint of change just around the corner.

Dr Desmond MacAuley, Medical Officer of Al Maktoum Hospital, vaccinating the public at Deira market, during an epidemic.

Bastakia on the threshold. Much of this area has been demolished during the last 30 years but some houses have been preserved, providing a satisfactory link with earlier times.

BADGEER, WHICH LITERALLY translated means windcatcher, was originally a Persian invention and is one of the earliest forms of air-conditioning. Once common throughout the lower Gulf, there are now few left as many of the old houses which they adorned have been pulled down to make way for modern development.

Of square construction, each tower is divided diagonally to form four triangular shafts. No matter from which direction the wind blows it will cause an increase in pressure on the windward side and a partial vacuum on the leeward. Thus air would be pushed down the tower before being sucked up again, creating a breeze through the room below. Often water would be thrown on the floor beneath the tower, the evaporation of which served to cool the house.

Windtowers also became a decorative feature with curlicues and cornices in a range of styles and patterns – the individual designs reflecting the style of the builder and the idiosyncrasies of the family.

Al Fahidi Fort, built around 180 years ago, has served various roles. Initially constructed as the main defence of the town, it subsequently became the seat of government, an ammunition store and jail. In 1971 Sheikh Rashid opened the restored fort as Dubai Museum which, much extended, it is still today.

Development in Deira. Nasr Square, which was originally spelt 'Nasser' as it was named in honour of the Egyptian president, is taking shape, but landmarks such as Deira Tower and BritishBank are still way in the future. Along the creek dhows still moor offshore, as they would continue to do until the land was reclaimed and the car parks and wharves built.

The varying designs of windtowers are well demonstrated in this photograph of the Bastakia area of Dubai, taken in 1976.

Sheikh Saeed's house before its restoration. Even in its then dilapidated state its classic lines and balanced proportions confer upon it an air of elegance and style. Sheikh Rashid prompted Noor Ali Rashid to visit his birthplace, accompanied by a Palace bodyguard, to photograph the crumbling yet still distinguishable remains.

AN ARCHITECTURAL HERITAGE. The attractive plaster-work panels that are such a distinctive feature of Dubai's old houses were not merely decorative. Combining aesthetic appeal with practicality, they were a means of ventilating a house without the loss of much-prized privacy – and enabled the occupants to observe the outside world without themselves being seen.

The panels often contain elements of traditional Islamic design together with other recurring themes – birds, flowers and coffee-pots were frequent features. Because they were made by hand rather than machine no two panels are identical, yet each contributes to a sense of harmony not only within the individual building but as a group in a complete neighbourhood.

Whilst many buildings have now been lost to the bulldozer several have been restored – notably Sheikh Saeed's house at Shindaga, with its ornate screens and cornices, fine majlis and broad verandas.

The strength of this door, leading to Al Fahidi Fort – now Dubai's Museum – is symbolic of the emirate's enduring heritage.

Sheikh Rashid after Eid prayers, accompanied by Ahmed Al Habtoor.

THROUGHOUT THE EMIRATES, in small villages, in towns and in the cities, the physical affirmation of the Muslim's deep faith is embodied in the mosques. New or old, plain or breathtakingly beautiful, their minarets, surmounted by the crescent, call the faithful to prayer five times a day. While the *muezzin* now no longer has to climb the tower to announce prayer time – modern amplification techniques take care of that – the cry of Allah O Akbar still echoes across the landscape.

Particularly for the visitor, especially one standing on the shore or by the creek, perhaps as a dhow slips silently by, the call of the *muezzin*, more than anything else, will sum up the feelings of Arabia, for the sound is the distilled essence of the land and its people.

The Friday mosque near Al Fahidi Fort and the Amiri Diwan in Bur Dubai.

Obaid Bel Jafflah outside Zabeel mosque.

IT HAD ALWAYS been easy for citizens of Dubai to meet with their Ruler through the majlis. Originally the only area of an Arab house which was open to male visitors, it is where guests are welcomed by the male members of the family. For the Sheikhs it became a place to which citizens would come to discuss business, air difficulties and seek resolution of disputes. At one time it was possible for anybody to attend a majlis but, as the country's population grew, more formal arrangements had to be made. Now a judicial system has removed the requirement for the Sheikh to have to arbitrate, and there are government departments to deal with matters such as land ownership. But the old tradition of open discussion remains and the Rulers of the Emirates are much closer to their people than those in most other parts of the world.

After Eid prayers, Sheikh Rashid would traditionally visit his elders – Mother, Father, Aunts, Uncles and siblings – after which he would go to Zabeel Palace where he would accept greetings from his people.

Sheikh Rashid with his uncle Sheikh Juma.

Sheikh Hasher Al Maktoum with his grandson, Sheikh Saeed bin Mohammed.

Sheikh Rashid with Sheikh Obaid bin Juma and young Sheikh Ahmed bin Saeed, now the Chairman of Emirates.

WEDDINGS PROVIDE THE occasion for some of the most joyous and colourful celebrations of all. The bride's house is often decorated with festoons of thousands of lights, feasts are held and the festivities can continue for several days. For members of prominent families the celebrations can extend way beyond family and friends – public entertainment frequently being arranged, including camel races, dances and musical performances to which all are invited.

In Dubai large areas were set aside for such public celebrations – the rows of wooden poles between which were strung lights looking like leafless forests when not in use.

Sheikh Maktoum's wedding in 1970. Sheikh Maktoum, Sheikh Mohammed and Sheikh Hamdan in deep discussion.

The house of Sheikh Khalifa bin Saeed Al Maktoum, the father of Sheikh Maktoum's bride, decorated in traditional style for the wedding.

Sheikh Juma bin Maktoum and Sheikh Hasher bin Maktoum were frequently received by Sheikh Maktoum at his residence at Zabeel.

IN KEEPING WITH the Islamic custom of ensuring that the rights of women are safeguarded, it is usual for a formal contract to be publicly agreed between bride and groom and, as in many other societies around the world, the bride-price forms an important part of the marriage covenant. Money, property or livestock is usually given by the groom to the father of the bride, who often passes this on to his daughter. Gifts of jewellery and clothes – and, traditionally, a handsome wooden chest decorated with brass fittings in which to keep them – are presents from the groom to the bride. Additionally, the husband-to-be pays for the cost of the food, music and other entertainment during the wedding celebrations.

But such mundane negotiations are forgotten during the festivities themselves when families and friends join together to celebrate the nuptials.

Bridegroom Sheikh Mohammed bin Khalifa Al Maktoum receiving congratulations from Sheikh Hamdan and Sheikh Mohammed on his wedding day.

Two and a half decades on: Sheikh Mohammed bin Khalifa Al Maktoum, second from the right, joins in heartily with the traditional dancing during the wedding of his own son, far right.

A fearless Sheikh Mohammed makes a gallant leap to another horse during a race, part of the celebratory events held on the occasion of Sheikh Maktoum's wedding.

THE CUSTOM OF the desert – in which dangerous territory the provision of food and drink to travellers would often mean the difference between life and death – lies at the core of Arab hospitality. Visitors are treated as honoured guests and whatever was available, often little enough, was shared with them.

On social visits that do not involve full meals visitors will usually be offered a selection of light refreshments – perhaps dates, sweet pastries, or vermicelli covered with honey or sugar. Before the more ready availability of fresh fruit in recent years the tinned variety would instead be offered, contemporary travellers often finding the slippery segments, steeped in syrup, difficult to capture!

Then, as now, the serving of coffee followed a traditional ritual. The *dallah* – the long-spouted brass coffee pot – would be used to pour the fragrant liquid into small, handleless cups which would be frequently refilled, although it was considered polite for no more than three cups to be consumed.

Brothers united: Noor Ali and his brother, Sultan Ali, strike formal poses behind the three royal siblings.

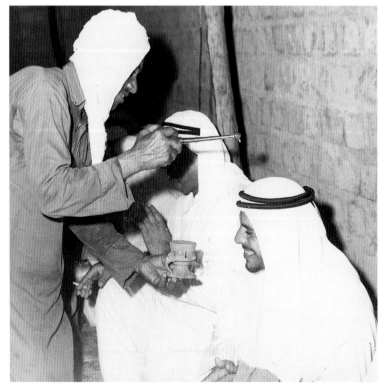

Noor Ali proudly hosted a dinner for Sheikh Maktoum and his brothers. Nothing but the best crystal, silver candelabra and fresh flowers for his distinguished guests.

The pleasant ritual of scattering rosewater is still prevalent in the UAE. Receiving this traditional custom is Khalaf Al Otaiba.

EIDS, WEDDINGS AND other festive occasions were often celebrated by gatherings at which traditional dances and songs were performed. Musical instruments reflect the materials available for their construction in years gone by – drums were made from animal skins stretched tightly over wooden frames and kept taut by warming them over braziers of hot charcoal, bagpipes were made from the stomach of a goat, and the *tamboura* – a stringed instrument somewhat like a harp but with a sound-box similar to that of a guitar – was of wood and skin.

Songs and dances draw not only on traditional Arabic themes, but have also absorbed Nubian and East African influences – areas with which the people of the emirates have had long trading links. Some of the more popular folk dances were the *naiashti*, in which colourfully dressed ladies swing their long hair in time to sweeping rhythms of drums and, sometimes, pipes; the *ardha*, a dance for men, to the beat of a tambourine-like drum; and the *razfa*, a complex routine in which two groups, singing alternate lines of folk songs, weave back and forth.

Festive music is still played on traditional instruments for many celebrations.

Mohammed Alabbar, second from the left, joins in a traditional male wedding dance.

Rhythmic chanting accompanied by the waving of camel sticks are a feature of many celebrations.

The Dubai of the 1960s must have been a place of endless fascination for young children – especially under the kindly tutelage of Freddy Luffman, the first British teacher in the city. Dubai's first infant school was founded by Bill Duff and Eric Tulloch in just one room near Shindaga in 1961. They later started the Dubai English Speaking School.

ALTHOUGH THREE SCHOOLS had opened in Dubai in the late 1930s, most children's education was restricted to reading, writing and simple mathematics and was usually obtained through the *mutawa* or religious teacher. Any further or more general tuition required travelling overseas – mainly to Bahrain, Iraq or Kuwait – and it wasn't until the opening of the first modern school in Dubai in 1957 that all-round education became available locally.

Education became a priority of the federation, at which time there were 147 schools in the Emirates with a total enrolment of 44,000 students. Just 20 years later that had grown to over 850 schools with 450,000 pupils.

Sheikh Rashid, accompanied by Political Agent Mr Craig and Political Resident Sir William Luce, joins Zahoudi Al Khatib, School Principal on an inspection of the school, which was located opposite Dubai Municipality. As the chalked blackboard reveals, the visit took place on 18 January, 1962.

Pupils don inked-on moustaches and beards in preparation for a performance during their school assembly.

Ladies of the Indian Association welcome Rajiv and Sonia Gandhi, on their way back from Iran during the Iran-Iraq conflict in January, 1990.

THE DOZENS OF different nationalities that flooded into Dubai as the economy grew brought with them their own social codes and habits. Tolerant as ever, Dubai was content to let them indulge in their own customs, pastimes and cuisine, which in turn has enriched the social and cultural life of the country. There can be few places of comparable size anywhere in the world that offer such diversity. As is so often the case with Dubai, the philosophy that 'if it's good for the people, it's good for Dubai' applies. For the most part expatriates have a genuine affection for the city and, because of this, they tend to put more into the place. Certainly for firms seeking to set up offices in the region the knowledge that they can employ happily settled people is of major importance.

The first ever foreign trade exhibition in Dubai was the Pakistan Exhibition, held by prominent Pakistani businessman and political figure, Ahmed Jaffer.

Spectators at a tennis match – a popular leisure pursuit with expats, but only when the cooler months made allowances for outdoor activities.

All set about with chrome finials, this handsome Chevy convertible – belonging to one of the Rulers – must have cut quite a dash on Dubai's roads. Certainly the chauffeur looks pretty proud of it.

FOR CENTURIES THE old way of life had changed little, the people's existence revolving around trading, fishing, pearling, the keeping of goats and camels and the tending of date palms. Capital was scarce and by and large the finance of development had to be met from the profits generated by enterprise.

Dubai had become the centre of the pearl trade for the whole of the Gulf with the arrival of the Persian merchants from Lingah. Many of the buyers came from India – much of the international business was controlled from Mumbai – forming part of the long association between the emirate and the sub-continent. Because of the structure of finance relating to the pearl trade, when it went into decline there were particularly hard times as substantial debts had to be paid off from scant resources.

The arrival of oil revenues enabled businesses to develop in a way that had been impossible before – and with it the way of life. Whilst many of the old traditions continued, new lifestyles evolved rapidly – and, as in other parts of the world, the car was to have an enormous effect.

A timeless scene – but the young boy was to see a world of opportunities unimaginable to the previous generation.

For millennia the camel had been the main means of transport – but now surfaced roads, lamp-posts and a whole gallimaufry of roundabouts, flyovers and traffic lights were to appear.

Sheikh Mohammed confidently leads the camel-racers forward to the starting line, watchful for the signal to begin.

In contrast to the fairly hazardous racing conditions of twenty years ago, this more recent event, with its modern fencing, lighting towers and jockeys equipped with safety helmets, proves that its organisers are much more safety-aware than their predecessors.

CAMEL-RACING, ORIGINALLY a method by which prospective buyers could test an animal's speed, strength and stamina, is keenly followed throughout the country. Whilst there are now specially-designed city racecourses complete with grandstands and car parks, in earlier times meetings were held on any convenient bit of desert, the track often marked by oil drums.

Before the arrival of the motor car the camel was the main means of transport for the people of the Arabian peninsula, its broad feet well adapted for walking through soft sand. With its ability to eat almost anything and to store water in its hump, the camel made long desert crossings possible and caravans from the area travelled as far as Jeddah, Damascus and the Yemen.

In recent years horse-racing has become a major sport in the emirate and the world's richest race, the Dubai World Cup, is held annually.

"To win a race like this in my own country, in front of my own people is special" announced Sheikh Mohammed on the occasion of winning the 1997 Dubai World Cup at Nad Al Shiba racecourse. Joining in with the congratulations, from the left: Ali Khamis Al Jafleh, Chairman of Dubai Racing Club, Sheikh Maktoum, Sheikh Saeed bin Maktoum and Sheikh Mohammed, lifting the shining trophy high above his head for all to see.

As with camel-races, spectators and owners would follow alongside the track in cars – an added dimension of excitement no longer possible at today's more formal courses. Sheikh Mohammed leaves a dusty trail as he leads the race.

Sheikh Maktoum bin Rashid.

DESPITE THE FACT that horses were never in common use in Dubai – their small hooves being less adapted to crossing sand than the broad-footed camel – the Arab horse is famous throughout the world. Indeed all racing thoroughbreds are descended from just three Arab horses introduced to Britain in the 18th century.

The Maktoum family, internationally known in the world of racing, own many of the sport's finest horses and regularly win some of the most prestigious races in the global calendar. The family has done much to encourage the breeding of thoroughbreds in Dubai, where many of their horses spend the winter.

Sheikh Hamdan bin Rashid.

Sheikh Mohammed bin Rashid.

Sheikh Ahmed bin Rashid.

Sheikh Maktoum meets a group of Bedouin who are preparing to participate in a camel-race.

Displays of riding skills provide an exciting spectacle at many meetings.

A DAY AT the races. Camels bred for racing receive meticulous care at the hands of their trainers who are expert in controlling the animals' diet and monitoring their exercise to improve their performance and stamina. Both male and female camels participate in races from around the age of four. Females usually retire at eight or ten years of age, but males often continue racing until as old as 15. Whilst there is no betting at either camel or horse-races, the latter offers substantial prizes to racegoers who can correctly forecast a run of six winners.

Races are also social affairs. In addition to regularly scheduled meetings there are special events to celebrate weddings and other occasions.

Races organised on the occasion of Sheikh Mohammed's wedding attracted an enthusiastic crowd.

Sheikh Rashid and Sheikh Zayed relax at a camel-race at Nad Al Shiba.

THE EMERGING STATE

A good crowd has turned out at Dubai's then new airport to welcome King Hussein of Jordan and watch the King and Sheikh Rashid take the salute.

Previous pages: The height of luxury – in 1960. The new airport with its runway of compacted sand was open from 0700 to 1300 daily.

The current departures terminal rises from the sand in this 1969 photograph.

THE FORERUNNER OF today's British Airways, Imperial Airways, inaugurated weekly services through Dubai in 1937. The airline rented premises for 5,280 rupees a year and paid a landing fee of 10 rupees for the Empire class flying boats which, en route from Cairo to Karachi, landed on the creek. During the Second World War the Horseshoe Route from South Africa to Australia via the Gulf and India brought more traffic and by 1944 there were eight flights a week through Dubai.

Work on Dubai's first airport suitable for regular flights by landplanes commenced in 1959. Located just four kilometres from the city centre on the site of the current airport, it was officially opened by Sheikh Rashid on 30 September, 1960. The 1,800-metre compacted sand runway was capable of handling aircraft up to the size of a DC-3 and, in its first full year of operation it handled 772 scheduled flights and some 10,000 passengers.

At Dubai Airport, a large crowd turns out to greet Sheikh Rashid, their popular leader, on his return from a foreign trip.

The new terminal building with its soaring pillars and distinctive curved walkways, opened in 1971.

A Douglas DC-3 Dakota of Gulf Aviation at Dubai Airport in the mid-60s. The most widely-used transport aircraft in the world, nearly 11,000 of the type were built. International Aeradio Ltd undertook air traffic control and aircraft handling duties at Dubai – with more rudimentary equipment than is now employed.

AS TRAFFIC GREW so the airport needed further expansion. The sand runway – which had a tendency to be blown away in the wash of an aircraft's propellers – was replaced by a 2,800-metre paved strip which, when completed in 1965, was capable of handling Boeing 707s and Vickers VC-10s, the largest passenger aircraft of the day. In 1969 work started on a new terminal building – the current departures terminal – which, with its 28-metre control tower and new apron, opened in 1971.

At the same time development of other infrastructural facilities was being undertaken – the extension of Port Rashid, new and improved roads, enhanced telecommunications services – together enabling Dubai to offer the modern fully integrated transport and communications structure demanded by the rapidly expanding business community.

Sheikh Ahmed, Chairman of Emirates with Sir Ralph Robins, Chairman of Rolls Royce on the occasion of signing an agreement to supply Rolls Royce engines for the Emirates fleet.

Sheikh Mohammed and Sheikh Hamdan prepare to receive oil company dignitaries at Dubai airport. Behind them construction of the extension that was to accommodate a new arrivals area was already underway.

The hijacked JAL Boeing 747 remained on the tarmac at Dubai for three days.

Army units remained at hand throughout the aircraft's enforced stay.

WHILST THE VOLUME of traffic through Dubai continued to grow it was not always of the welcome kind. On 20 July, 1973 a Japan Airlines Boeing 747 was hijacked and forced to land at Dubai. For the three days and nights that it remained stranded Defence Minister Sheikh Mohammed led the teams of negotiators round the clock, before the aircraft eventually left for Damascus with hijackers and passengers. Barely four months later Sheikh Mohammed was once again called to the airport – this time to deal with the hijackers of a KLM Boeing 747 with 247 passengers on board. The aircraft left soon afterwards for Aden, but returned to Dubai when permission to land was refused. Prolonged negotiations followed which resulted in the hijackers' surrender.

Medical assistance at the ready.

Soldiers finding some respite from the relentless July sun.

Sheikhs waiting to greet a foreign head of state.

THERE WERE HAPPIER comings and goings at the airport. As international trade grew, so diplomatic, commercial and social links developed. Increasingly, Dubai was visited by heads of state and other dignitaries, from both the Arab world and nations further afield; business people came to further their interests in one of the world's fastest-growing economies; and friends and relatives of residents came on visits to see for themselves the place about which they had heard so much.

The growth was reflected in the airport's statistics. At the beginning of the 1970s there were 14 airlines connecting Dubai to some 30 destinations with 210 flights per week; by the end of the decade there were 34 airlines serving 60 destinations with 1,024 flights per week.

Sheikh Rashid, emerging from a flight, was always greeted by a throng of photographers and press upon his return from a foreign trip.

Sheikh Rashid and a reception party prepare to greet Sheikh Isa off the plane, on one of his many visits to Dubai.

DUBAI, BOTH AS an entity in its own right as well as a member of the United Arab Emirates, has played an increasingly prominent role in Middle Eastern affairs as well as on a wider world stage. Federally, the nation has diplomatic ties with more than 120 countries around the globe, handled through over 40 embassies, consulates and other missions. The country is also a member of the United Nations, the Gulf Co-operation Council, the Islamic Conference Organisation, OPEC and the Arab League, as well as many other international organisations.

Such active participation in international and regional matters has led to state and private visits from the leaders of many nations, furthering mutual understanding and opening new opportunities for trade and cultural exchanges.

Sheikh Mohammed with Mikhail Gorbachev, then President of the USSR.

Abdul Jalil Yousuf Darwish, BritishBank Executive Director and CEO – UAE during a reception held in honour of Lady Margaret Thatcher.

Sheikh Maktoum and Nawaz Sharif, Prime Minister of Pakistan.

Sheikh Rashid receives King Faisal of Saudi Arabia at Zabeel Palace. Also attending the reception: the late Sheikh Khalid bin Mohammed Al Qasimi of Sharjah; Sheikh Saqr bin Mohammed Al Qassimi of Ras Al Khaimah and Sheikh Rashid bin Humaid Al Nuaimi of Ajman.

PARTICULARLY CLOSE TIES exist between the countries of the Gulf Co-operation Council – whose members are Kuwait, Saudi Arabia, Bahrain, Qatar and Oman as well as the United Arab Emirates. In the negotiations that had led to the formation of the UAE there had been lengthy discussions not only between the emirates but also with Bahrain and Qatar. Although the latter two had eventually decided to become independent countries, the close contacts that had been established between the states of the Gulf in the period leading up to federation were maintained – and helped, ten years later, in the formation of the Gulf Co-operation Council.

India, with whom Dubai had for so long been trading – and, going back to the times before Indian independence, from where the British administered the Trucial States – has always had a special relationship with the region. And Pakistan, created in 1947 in the partition of India, has especially close ties reinforced by the mutual Muslim heritage.

Sheikh Rashid and Sheikh Sabah Al-Ahmad Al-Sabah, Kuwait's Foreign Minister.

Sheikh Maktoum with the late Prime Minister of
India, Indira Gandhi.

Sheikh Maktoum and Sheikh Hamdan with the late
President of Pakistan, Zia-ul-Haq.

NOT ALL ARRIVALS came on such stately visits. Quite apart from official links with other countries Dubai was also developing common bonds through a wide range of cultural and sporting activities. From basketball to bowling, cricket to rugby, skydiving to dinghy sailing, sportsmen in Dubai, both nationals and expatriates, were making their mark on the world stage – and their competitors were equally keen to visit for a return match.

As these relationships developed Dubai embarked on sponsorship of events in other countries as well as providing world-class facilities on its own territory – leading to the city's current position as the sporting capital of the entire Gulf region.

Mohi-din Binhendi, Dubai's Director-General of Civil Aviation, greets the greatly admired actress Vijayantimala and Dr Bali on their arrival in Dubai.

Pakistan's cricket captain, Imran Khan, now a political figure.

Sheikh Rashid bin Mohammed is presented with a racing award by Britain's Princess Anne at Nad Al Shiba.

THE OLD
ORDER PASSETH

Sheikh Rashid – extraordinarily combining the attributes of visionary with those of a shrewd merchant – was the architect of Dubai's remarkable development and success.

Sheikh Maktoum bin Rashid Al Maktoum, Ruler of Dubai, UAE Vice-President and Prime Minister.

Previous pages: Sheikh Maktoum, Sheikh Hamdan and Sheikh Mohammed.

IN DUBAI, AS in the other emirates, for more than a hundred years successive Rulers had combined autocracy on the one hand with a patriarchal near-democracy on the other, holding power under the principle of 'first amongst equals', and maintaining their positions by virtue of their accomplishments. It was not unusual, if a Ruler failed to provide the leadership that the country needed, for a more able chieftain to be acknowledged by the population.

The traditional system had worked well in the less complex environment of the pre-oil era but Sheikh Rashid appreciated that the developing emirate required a method of government more suited to the changing needs of the times. And, as is customary in the Gulf, it was first to his family that he turned.

Sheikh Hamdan bin Rashid Al Maktoum, Deputy Ruler of Dubai and UAE Finance and Industry Minister.

Sheikh Mohammed bin Rashid Al Maktoum, Crown Prince of Dubai and UAE Defence Minister.

A meeting of Dubai Municipality. From left to right: Sheikh Rashid, his legal advisor, Adi Al Bitar, Sheikh Mohammed and Sheikh Maktoum. Sheikh Rashid's sons regularly attended these meetings and developed a shrewd understanding of business matters from such discussions.

THE REMARKABLE DEVELOPMENT of Dubai had required an adaptation of the traditional methods of administration, bringing both responsibility and power to a new generation. The old order recalled the Greek city-state's ideal of democracy: communities small enough for each member to be able to have access to the ruler; close-knit so that each citizen knew most of his fellows; self-disciplining for the same reason; and offering exile as the only solution for those dissidents who found it impossible to live within the commonly accepted framework. But rapid population growth and the sophisticated systems needed to successfully administer a complex modern state required a new approach.

Here military exercises at Manama in Ajman are observed by the Rulers of Dubai, Abu Dhabi, Umm Al Quwain and Ras Al Khaimah.

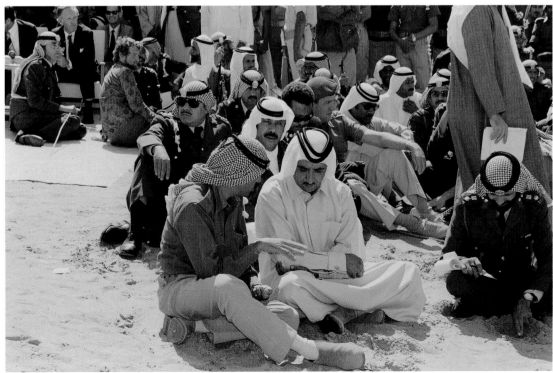

Sheikh Maktoum attending army manoeuvres at Manama.

MUCH OF THE work involved in setting up the ministries and other apparatus of state fell on Sheikh Rashid's sons, Sheikh Maktoum, Sheikh Hamdan and Sheikh Mohammed. Additionally, inter-emirate co-operation, fostered under the Trucial States Council which was founded in 1952, reached maturity with the formation of the UAE. Whilst the two architects of the federation, Sheikh Zayed and Sheikh Rashid, had agreed on the fundamental structure of the union, it was to senior members of their families that they entrusted the task of implementation.

Sheikh Maktoum and Sheikh Mohammed.

Brothers in arms: Pictured here in a relaxed and warm embrace at a private luncheon hosted by Noor Ali Rashid, the close bond between the three royal siblings is clearly apparent.

Sheikh Hamdan and Sheikh Mohammed in discussion.

Sheikh Rashid at the opening of the
road tunnel under the Clock Tower
roundabout.

SHEIKH RASHID, ALTHOUGH Ruler
since acceding on the death of his father
Sheikh Saeed bin Maktoum in 1958, had
taken a leading role in the affairs of the
emirate from a young age – and had been,
in effect, Sheikh Saeed's Regent from 1939.
Certainly the phenomenal rise in Dubai's
prosperity was principally due to his
commercial acumen. Immediately after his
accession he instituted the Municipal Council
(the forerunner of the Municipality), engaged
a firm of town planners to draw up a master
plan for the development of the city,
arranged for a survey to be undertaken in
quest of an improved water supply, initiated
the formation of the police force and set
about the construction of the first airstrip.

Throughout his life, Sheikh Rashid
pledged all his time to the development of
Dubai; even during vacations, he was
known to seek the best advice, source new
contractors, and initiate new ventures for
the emirate's future.

This occasion marked the last time
the Dubai population was to see
Sheikh Rashid before his long illness.

Striking an official pose: Sheikh Rashid – this is
Noor Ali Rashid's personal favourite from his broad
collection of portraits of Dubai's former Ruler.

WHILST DUBAI HAS a close association with all the emirates that go to make up the UAE, there are particularly strong ties with Abu Dhabi. Historically the ruling families are from the same tribe, the Bani Yas, which has several sub-sections. Amongst these are the Al Bu Falah branch, whose home was the Liwa oasis in what is now the emirate of Abu Dhabi, and which includes the house of Al Nahyan, whose dynasty has uninterruptedly ruled Abu Dhabi since at least the early eighteenth century; and the Rawashid, the largest sub-section of the Bani Yas, which includes the Al Bu Falasa. In 1833 a dispute arose between these branches and the Al Bu Falasa moved to Dubai, establishing an independent state which has been ruled by the Maktoum family ever since.

Sheikh Rashid and Sheikh Zayed at Sheikh Zayed's Palace in Dubai before federation.

Sheikh Maktoum presiding over the first cabinet meeting in Abu Dhabi in 1971.

Sheikh Mohammed and
Sheikh Zayed quietly confer during
Eid greetings in February, 1997.

Sheikh Rashid offers a fatherly
embrace as a sign of his great
affection for and bond with Sheikh
Maktoum, to whom he taught all the
principles of strong leadership and
diligence to serve the people.

A traditional meal shared amongst friends and business colleagues. From the far left: Abdul Rehman Al Ghurair, Ahmed Moosa, Abdullah Al Ghurair, Sheikh Hasher Al Maktoum, Sheikh Ahmed Al Maktoum, Sheikh Butti Al Maktoum and Khalifa Mohammed Kraif.

ASTUTE, DECISIVE AND charismatic, Sheikh Rashid was a formidable personality indeed. From long before federation he had played a prominent part in establishing contacts between the Rulers of the individual states and encouraging a sense of common purpose to be developed. He also assembled a team of experts in a variety of fields to help in the development of the emirate. Combining the foresight of a visionary with the shrewdness of a trader he applied both talents in full measure and it is true to say that the startlingly successful progress of Dubai from the 1950s through until his death in 1990 was largely attributable directly to him.

But his determination to create a modern state did not alter the fundamental tenets of the community. The traditional importance of the family, the custom of hospitality and the care for the less fortunate members of society remained – as they do still today.

Sheikh Rashid with his youngest son, Sheikh Ahmed.

Those foreign visitors who received invitations to dine with the royal family would quietly exclaim at the abundance of dishes offered to them. Moreover, they were intrigued by the Arabic tradition of eating with the hand, and indeed welcomed this respite from the staunch conventions of Western table manners.

THE GENERATION OF leaders that followed have maintained the same spirit of goodwill, tolerance, understanding and cordial co-operation established by Sheikh Rashid. From an early age they had been prepared for the positions of responsibility that would one day become theirs. Sheikh Maktoum succeeded his father as UAE Vice-President and Prime Minister, and Ruler of Dubai. Other members of the family have also assumed the responsibilities of leadership, with Sheikh Hamdan becoming Minister of Finance and Industry and Sheikh Mohammed Minister of Defence.

The Maktoum family have provided the leadership, encouragement, continuity and conditions that have enabled the people of the emirate to use to the full their commercial skills. And, in keeping with tradition, a new generation of leaders is being groomed to guide the emirate through the changing times of the new century.

Sheikh Rashid with his grandson Sheikh Saeed bin Maktoum at Sheikh Mohammed's wedding.

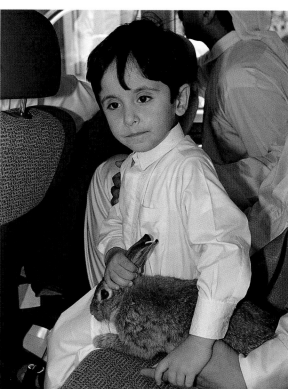

A new generation arising. Sheikh Hamdan's son with his pet rabbit.

Sheikh Maktoum's eldest son, Sheikh Saeed (also pictured as a child, top left), with Sheikh Mohammed.

Sheikh Mohammed bin Maktoum Al Maktoum seated in the Royal Box at Nad Al Shiba racecourse.

Sheikh Maktoum with
Majid Al Futtaim, who since the
mid-50s has been known as 'Japan's
ambassador', due to the amount of
trade between the two countries his
agencies – from electronics to
watches – have generated.

From left to right: Sultan Saqr Al
Suwaidi; Tariam Omran Tariam;
Qasim Sultan receiving the Sultan
Al Owais award on behalf of Dubai
Municipality; Sultan Ali Al Owais;
Mohammed Al Murr and
Saeed Hareb.

AND SO THE story continues. From an obscure entrepôt port to a major centre of transhipment and trade; from a dusty desert landing strip to the busiest airport in the region; from small souks lining sandy alleyways to modern malls that host the Dubai Shopping Festival; from the occasional camel-race amongst the dunes to the venue of a series of world-class sporting events; from unsurfaced tracks to a network of super-highways, Dubai's development has been extraordinary by any standards, accomplishing all this in little more than a generation.

Yet, amidst all this change, there are constants too, not the least of those being the continuity supplied by the Maktoum family who, for several generations, have provided the leadership, encouragement and conditions that have enabled the people of the emirate to use their commercial skills to the full.

Mohamed Alabbar, Director-General, Dubai Department of Economic Development, presents former US President George Bush with a commemorative gold coin, during a luncheon hosted by Citibank in Dubai. The bank's General Manager, Ahmed Bin Brek, looks on.

Overleaf: The creek's waters never stilled, but constantly lapped against the hull of boats that negotiated their way down its wide channel. Either for trading purposes or as a more leisurely pursuit, the lure of raising a boat's mainsail and charting the vessel into wind was too great an opportunity to miss.

Gathered at the Dubai Chamber of Commerce and Industry, from right: Saeed Al Nabooda, Sheikh Mohammed bin Rashid, Dr Khalifa bin Mohammed Sulaiman, Qasim Sultan and Hassan Al Shaikh.